Original title:
Leaves of Joy

Copyright © 2025 Creative Arts Management OÜ
All rights reserved.

Author: Dorian Ashford
ISBN HARDBACK: 978-1-80581-873-1
ISBN PAPERBACK: 978-1-80581-400-9
ISBN EBOOK: 978-1-80581-873-1

Coronet of Colors

In the garden where giggles grow,
Bouncing blooms put on a show.
Twirling petals with a bright hue,
Each one whispers, "Guess who?"

Dandelions prance in the breeze,
Tickled by a swarm of bees.
Tulips joke with a cheeky grin,
"We always lose, but we'll still win!"

Heartbeats of the Earth

Bouncing bugs with tiny shoes,
Waltz around in morning dew.
Worms have parties underground,
In the soil, fun's always found!

Squirrels flip in a silly dance,
Nuts in paws, they twirl and prance.
Frogs in ponds sing out loud,
Jumping high to tease the cloud!

Serenity Unfolds

A butterfly trips on a breeze,
Wondering where to tease the trees.
"Tag! You're it!" it seems to play,
Spinning joy in sunny sway.

Clouds pretend to spill a drink,
Laughter tumbles, causing a wink.
Rainbows chuckle from above,
Saying, "Hey, we all just love!"

Radiance of the Day

Sunbeams dance on cheeky grass,
Tickling toes as they pass.
Everyone's smiling, oh so bright,
Color splashes in pure delight!

Merry shadows play hide and seek,
Swaying to the rhythm, cheek to cheek.
With giggles echoing all around,
In this funny world, joy is found!

Radiant Motions in the Green

In a dance of color, they twirl,
Whirling around in a leafy swirl.
Silly squirrels in their little hats,
Playing tag with flamboyant spats.

Nature giggles in shades of bright,
Sunlight bounces, a joyful sight.
The wind joins in with a breezy spin,
As critters and blooms share a cheeky grin.

Celebration in the Forest's Heart

In the heart of the woods, a party's planned,
Bashful bunnies hop, their feet all tanned.
Dancing mushrooms sway to the beat,
While ants serve snacks, a delightful treat.

The raccoons jive in their tuxedo best,
While owls wear glasses, look quite impressed.
A chorus of birds sings silly tunes,
As flowers sway under the watchful moons.

Blossoms of Lively Whimsy

Poppin' petals with a burst of cheer,
Tickling the toes of all who draw near.
Bouncing butterflies, in colors galore,
Whispering secrets from flower to floor.

Giggles echo from tree branch to tree,
As frogs play leapfrog, full of glee.
A breeze tells jokes, quite quick and spry,
While daisies make crowns that reach for the sky.

The Vibrant Symphony of Growth

An orchestra tunes with a harp made of vines,
While whimsical creatures sip sweetened wines.
The beat of the soil, a rhythm divine,
As crickets chirp, saying, 'Let's all shine!'

Chortling pines with their ticklish bark,
Join in the laugh from dawn until dark.
A parade of sprouts march with great flair,
Each step a giggle, each wiggle a care.

Delighted Dances in a Gentle Breeze

In the park, a squirrel skips,
Chasing winds with little nips.
A dog with style, does a twirl,
While kids just giggle, watch and whirl.

Tree branches swing, a playful tune,
Chirping birds in bright festoon.
Tiptoeing ants, they strut their grace,
Underfoot, they own the place.

Nature's Palette of Exuberance

Bright flowers wear their polka dots,
Bouncing bees on funny plots.
Clouds like pillows in the sky,
Tickle the sun, making it sigh.

The river chats with giggly streams,
Planning mischief with the beams.
Frogs hop in their raincoat suits,
Croaking jests while eating roots.

A Tapestry of Grateful Shimmers

The daisies gossip, share a laugh,
While butterflies dance, a bubbly staff.
A cat with shades poses so cool,
While rabbits discuss their own school.

Beetles hold a tiny parade,
Marching on, unafraid.
A grasshopper does a little flip,
As daisies cheer and tightly grip.

Sunshine's Touch on Waving Iris

Sunshine sneezes, petals sway,
With joyful bounces, come what may.
Worms exchange their silly jokes,
While sleepy snails on leaf beds soak.

A dandelion poofs with glee,
Seeds like dreams float wild and free.
Hopping frogs beg for a tune,
In this garden, filled with June.

Embracing the Warmth

The sun beamed down, a golden throne,
Where birds danced round on a whimsy phone.
Each ray tickled, with laughter it tickles,
On cheeks like apples, oh what sweet giggles!

The grass wore hats of daisies bright,
Swaying around, quite the silly sight.
A breeze blew pants of gusty flair,
While squirrels joined in a raucous affair!

Nature's Sweet Serenade

A frog once croaked a choosy tune,
That made the flowers sway and swoon.
With bees in shades that buzz like cheer,
And ants on stage, did I hear a jeer?

The trees all gossip in leafy tones,
Whispering jokes through creaky bones.
Each rustle shared a secret cheer,
As nature giggled, can you hear?

Fluttering Hopes

A butterfly wearing polka dots,
Flits through gardens, gives it hot shots.
Chasing sunbeams with flapping glee,
Leaves a trail, oh look at me!

The flowers shimmy, what a wild dance,
Enticing all with a wobbly prance.
Bees buzz a tune, weaving the air,
While daisies trade quips without a care!

The Palette of Happiness

Colors splash in a whimsical fight,
Pinks and yellows feel just so bright.
A painter tosses hues like confetti,
Nature wears joy, looking so petty.

Giggles erupt from clouds up high,
A rainbow stretches, oh me, oh my!
The world a canvas, smiles in frame,
Who knew laughter could be so tame?

Whispers of Happy Branches

In a tree where giggles grow,
Squirrels offer quite the show.
Chasing acorns, oh what fun,
Nature's jest has just begun.

Branches bend with laughter true,
Birds join in with songs anew.
Winds carry jokes through the air,
Tickling leaves with playful flair.

Dance of Sunlit Petals

Petals twirl in bright delight,
Waltzing under beams of light.
Bee in bow tie, buzzing fast,
A floral fest, a riotous blast.

Butterflies in polka dots,
Fluttering with silly plots.
Every bloom a comic tale,
Nature's vaudeville, never stale.

Bright Tides of Nature's Laughter

Ripples giggle on the pond,
Frogs jump high, of that they're fond.
Sunshine dances on the waves,
While nature pranks, its whim behaves.

Crickets chirp in silly rhymes,
Tickling grass through all the climes.
The world chuckles in its glee,
A joyful riot, wild and free.

Fluttering Echoes of Bliss

Butterflies with silly grins,
Chase their tails in playful spins.
Dandelions float like dreams,
Laughing in the sunlit beams.

The brook bubbles, quite the tease,
Whispering jokes with every breeze.
Every turn a laughter shared,
In this world, no heart is scared.

Echoes of Laughter

In the garden, flowers twirl,
Bouncing like a happy girl.
Squirrels steal a snack or two,
While the sun shines bright and blue.

Bumblebees do silly dances,
Chasing butterflies in glances.
Every giggle makes a sound,
Echoes of joy all around.

The breeze plays tricks, gives a shove,
Twirling hats, a game of love.
Clouds above, they cheer and play,
As we laugh the hours away.

Puddles form from sudden rain,
Wiggle-walks to dodge the drain.
Laughter leaps in every heart,
Nature's stage, a funny art.

The Magic of Togetherness

Friends assemble, what a sight,
Pizza slices, pure delight.
Jokes exchanged, we share our glee,
Belly laughs, like bumblebees.

Chasing shadows, we all trip,
Trip and tumble, fall and flip.
Side by side, we dance and spin,
Every loss becomes a win.

In this chaos, sparks ignite,
Cups of joy, we raise tonight.
Games of tag and hide-and-seek,
Every laugh, a treasure peak.

Stars above start winking down,
Lighting up our playful town.
Together, fun's our greatest treasure,
In every giggle, boundless pleasure.

Whispered Joys

In the rustle, secrets hide,
Trees lean close, they whisper wide.
What's the joke? A riddle spun,
Tickled tongues, we laugh and run.

Silly faces, grand charades,
Frogs in hats on leafy blades.
Every chuckle, bubbles rise,
Rippling laughter, soaring skies.

Sunset paints a funny scene,
Pinks and oranges, bold and keen.
Nature giggles, paints its cheer,
Whispers of fun draw us near.

As fireflies light up the night,
The world is filled with pure delight.
Each tiny spark, a laugh's embrace,
In whispered joys, we find our place.

Serenade of the Seasons

Springtime bursts with blooms galore,
Bouncing bunnies hop and roar.
Crisp leaves crunch beneath our feet,
Funny faces, sunny greet.

Summer sun brings ice cream drips,
Wiggly dances, summer trips.
Sweaty brows, we laugh and sigh,
Kites go crashing in the sky.

Autumn's here with swirling gusts,
Pumpkin hats and silly busts.
Falling leaves do pirouettes,
Who knew joy had no regrets?

Winter wraps us snug and tight,
Snowball fights in frosty light.
Laughter echoes through the chill,
Each season brings its joyful thrill.

Emotions in Bloom

With giggles fresh as morning air,
Petals dance without a care.
Silly whispers, bright and light,
Laughter blooms, a pure delight.

Tickled by the sun's warm rays,
We frolic through our playful days.
Each chuckle paints a vibrant scene,
Joyful antics, evergreen.

Kissed by Morning Dew

Waking up with silly glee,
Dewdrops spark, just wait and see.
A grasshopper sings, hopping high,
As birds do their own salsa fly.

Giggles drip from leaves above,
Nature's wink is full of love.
In puddles, mirrors of pure cheer,
Splashing laughter, crystal clear.

Secrets of the Heart

Whispers tickle tender ears,
Behind each smile, there's no fears.
A wink and grin, oh what a tease,
Heartfelt secrets dance with ease.

In corners where the shadows play,
Laughter hides, but won't decay.
Jokes unfold like petals bright,
Giggling through the silent night.

A Canvas of Smiles

Brushstrokes of laughter fill the air,
Every frown transformed with flair.
A canvas painted in pure fun,
Where every laugh says, 'We've won!'

Splatters of joy, puddles wide,
Colors mixing side by side.
Art of giggles, bright and bold,
In this masterpiece, dreams unfold.

The Reflective Soul

In the park, I see my face,
A squirrel gives me quite the chase.
He thinks my snack is all his due,
While I just want a quiet view.

With every step, a crunch and crack,
I tripped and fell; oh, what a knack!
The birds all laugh, they cannot hide,
As I roll forward with pride wide.

Each gust of wind, a playful tease,
My reflection dances with such ease.
A game of tag with trees so tall,
I wonder who will win this brawl.

So here I sit, a thoughtful pose,
Nature's prankster, as wisdom grows.
With giggles bubbling like a brook,
I guess I'll stay—let's take a look.

Wandering Heartstrings

A breeze whirls with a cheeky grin,
It tickles my nose, oh where have I been?
The flowers wink, a colorful show,
Who knew they'd hog the spotlight so?

I spotted a gnome, he's grinning wide,
With feet so big, how's he even tried?
He nods at me, my confidant rare,
Together we plot, with mischief to share.

A floaty bug swings near my head,
I dance with it, it's quite a spread!
The sunbeams giggle, the skies applaud,
For pure silly fun, I'm never flawed.

So here I wander, heart a-flutter,
In this funny realm, I'll never stutter.
With every wink and whimsical chase,
I embrace the joy in this wild place.

Celestial Floral Whispers

A dandelion floats, a wish on a flight,
I grabbed for it fast, oh what a sight!
It popped in my hand like a starburst treat,
Giving my fingers a fluffy sweet beat.

The daisies giggle, they're plotting a game,
In a floral twist, they call out my name.
With petals like confetti, they burst into cheer,
As bees snap selfies, they're quite the queer.

An umbrella mushroom holds court in the shade,
With jokes about toast, it's quite the charade.
I laugh till I cry, rolling on the ground,
In a kingdom of giggles, where joy can be found.

So let's paint the garden with laughter and cheer,
As cosmic blooms whisper—stay a while here.
With each playful sigh, life spins in delight,
In this whimsical realm, everything feels right.

Floating on Air

Bouncing like a ball, so light,
Up, up, I soar, what a sight!
Twisting in the breeze, I fly,
Giggles echo, oh my, oh my!

Up in the clouds, I play tag,
With silly birds and a wagging rag.
Chasing the sun, so warm and bright,
Floating on air, what pure delight!

A tumble here, a wiggle there,
Laughter bubbles, fills the air.
With every squawk, a funny dance,
In this skyward, playful prance!

A flip, a spin, a cloud to chase,
Cheerful smiles on every face.
Oh the joy, it's everywhere,
Floating on air, without a care!

Harmony's Embrace

A melody of chuckles near,
Laughter twirls, the skies are clear.
Swaying trees join in the fun,
Dancing shadows, everyone!

Ticklish breezes lift the day,
As critters join the grand ballet.
Each rustle sings a playful tune,
In harmony beneath the moon.

Jumpy squirrels in a race,
Chasing giggles, a furry chase.
They tumble, roll, and spin around,
In this jolly joy abound!

Together here, with playful cheer,
In this embrace, we all appear.
With every laugh, a quirky face,
Join the fun in harmony's grace!

The Veil of Elation

Underneath a mystic veil,
Whirls of joy in a grand scale.
A bubble here, a splash of glee,
With each twist, wild and free!

The skies burst forth in wild delight,
As chortles bounce from morn to night.
A wink, a grin, a silly glance,
Caught in this whimsical dance.

Hide and seek with the autumn breeze,
Catching giggles like buzzing bees.
In every turn, a quirky sight,
Wrapped in joy, the world feels right!

The veil lifts, and what do we see?
A parade of laughs, a jubilee.
In every nook, sweet laughter's drawn,
The elation dances on the lawn!

Rippled Reflections

In ponds where giggles softly play,
Ripples bounce in a frolicsome way.
Reflecting smiles on water's face,
Nature's joke in this silly space.

Frogs croak puns, and ducklings quack,
In a world where joy won't lack.
Each splash is laughter's brilliant tune,
Together under the cheeky moon.

With every ripple, joy takes wing,
Joking fish in a watery fling.
Swirls of fun as the sun dips low,
Silly antics steal the show!

So join the jive, come splash around,
In this watery dance that knows no bound.
Each chuckle's echoed, round and round,
In rippled reflections, joy is found!

The Rapture of Moments

In the park, we dance with glee,
A squirrel steals lunch from me.
The sun shines bright, a silly hat,
While pigeons plot—how rude is that!

Laughter echoes, skies are blue,
Jumping jacks in goofy shoes.
Chasing dreams on bouncing feet,
We'll celebrate with doughnut treats!

Giddy giggles, tickled toes,
In playful pranks, adventure grows.
We leap and spin, oh what a sight,
In this rapture, pure delight!

With floppy hats and joy in store,
We wave goodbye, but crave some more.
Tomorrow's fun, a brand-new play,
To chase the clouds—we'll find our way.

Fading into Bliss

A coffee spill, my favorite shirt,
The laughter flows; it doesn't hurt.
I trip on air and then I grin,
Even clumsiness is a win!

Picnic antics on the grass,
We tossed the salad, let it pass!
With ants in line for crumbs we leave,
Their little march, what a reprieve!

A toaster battle, toast flying high,
Jelly sticks like glue on the fly.
We create art, a masterpiece,
Fading colors, laughter's feast!

As dusk approaches, stars will peek,
We'll dance the night, 'til we can't speak.
In fading light, our spirits rise,
What foolish joy, beneath the skies!

Unfolding Wonder

A kite that soars and twirls with flair,
Chasing the wind through tousled hair.
Unexpected rain, a splashy cheer,
A muddy puddle, oh my dear!

The ice cream melts, a sticky fate,
Whipped cream goggles, we celebrate.
In silly hats, we prance about,
Who knew joy could make us shout!

A game of tag, we chase the sun,
Dizzy circles, oh what fun!
We dance with shadows, giggles loud,
In this wonder, we feel so proud.

Under the moon, we whisper dreams,
With fizzling sparks and laughter's beams.
Unfolding marvels, the night is bright,
A symphony of joy takes flight!

The Tender Path

On a quirky route, we wander free,
Dodging puddles, just you and me.
Silly signs, like "Bunny Crossing,"
We stop to ponder, laughing, tossing.

Unexpectedly, a twirling leaf,
Catches our eyes; what a disbelief!
We chase it round, a fluttering jest,
A game of giggles, we are blessed.

A hidden treasure—a wormy prize,
In muddy boots, we claim the skies.
With each stumble, we learn to glide,
On the tender path, let's take the ride.

At twilight's end, our hearts aglow,
With every laugh, a gentle flow.
This silly journey, hand in hand,
On this tender path, we make our stand!

Feathered Joys

Round and round the chickens trot,
Clucking tales of what they've got.
Feathers flying in the breeze,
A chicken dance among the trees.

Pigs roll in mud, adorned with glee,
Trying to find the best spot to be.
With oinks and snorts, they join the fray,
And dance like it's the best of days.

Splash of Euphoria

A duck with shades, a sunny hat,
Waddling quick, looking like that.
Jumping puddles, such a thrill,
As frogs croak out, 'We've got skill!'

The squirrel's juggling acorns, watch!
With nutty moves that hit the spot.
Who knew woodland critters had flair?
Their comedy pulls you from despair.

Tranquil Traces

Butterflies wear polka-dot ties,
Birds tweet songs with silly highs.
The sunbeams giggle on the green,
While crickets wear their best routine.

A snail slides by in a fancy shell,
Laughing at his slow, grand swell.
With each tiny step, oh what a show,
A race with time, but he's in the flow.

Horizon of Hope

A horizon where the silly dance,
Wiggle and twirl, take a chance!
Clouds puff cheeks in fluffy shapes,
As giggles bounce like silly drapes.

The sun winks down, a playful tease,
Its rays tickle like a summer breeze.
Joyfully bursting, colors in flight,
Creating hilarity, pure delight.

Festive Shimmers of Earth's Canvas

Colors dance on the ground,
While squirrels play hide and seek.
Nature's confetti, all around,
With laughter echoing, so unique.

Giggles foxtrot with the breeze,
As acorns tumble, making noise.
The world's a stage with comic tease,
Every flutter brings such joys.

Beneath the trees, a jester's game,
In autumn's hat, they spin about.
Oh what a fun and silly claim,
That puddles turn to giggling clouts!

Sunny rays, a playful sight,
As shadows prance beneath the cheer.
In nature's play, hearts take flight,
Just like a dance, let's all adhere.

The Glimmer of Happiness in Each Leaf

A rustle hints at jokes untold,
As branches sway to rhythms sweet.
Their whispers weave a tale so bold,
Of chipmunk antics, oh what a treat!

Dancing colors, oh what a sight,
Donning hats of vibrant hue.
Every flicker, pure delight,
As laughter spills like morning dew.

Who knew a gust could cause such cheer?
With nature's glee, there's room for play.
Twirling rays bring warmth so near,
Turning mundane to a cabaret!

In this grand show, we laugh and tease,
As the wind tickles with gentle glee.
For every rustle, joy finds ease,
In the circus of the carefree.

Whispers of Laughter

Whispers flit on golden wings,
As breezes tinkle through the boughs.
A bouquet of giggles softly sings,
While nature celebrates the vows.

Jumpy joes with acorn hats,
Tumble and bounce in silly spree.
Laughter bubbles from fluffy cats,
As they chase twirling leaves, so free.

Even the trees wear grins today,
In this flip-flop of joyful hues.
Each awkward twist leads us to play,
Where laughter blooms like morning snooze.

Oh, how the world in jest does spin,
With mischief tangled in the air.
Nature's chuckles find their kin,
In this merry play, without a care!

Harvest of Serenity

In meadows bright, the good vibes flow,
With giggles popping like sweetcorn sprout.
Nature's fair, a wild show,
Where every crown is twisted out.

Bouncing bugs in jolly race,
Chasing shadows, just for fun.
Sun-kissed cheeks light up each face,
As laughter sails, the day is won!

Each frolic echoes in the air,
With chirping birds in friendly brawl.
From rustling grass, joy's everywhere,
In this serene, silly free-for-all.

Bring out the cake and sing a tune,
For nature's gift, it brings us cheer.
Beneath the sun and silver moon,
It's all a harvest full of cheer!

The Color of Cheerful Breezes

A flutter here, a giggle there,
Bright shades dance without a care.
Swaying along with silly glee,
Nature's laughter, wild and free.

Brushes of orange, splashes of green,
What a sight, it's quite the scene!
Whispers of pastel, tickling the air,
Who knew color could wear such flair?

Tell me a secret in the breeze,
How do you tickle such tall trees?
With hues of happiness, oh so bright,
They twirl and swirl 'til the fall of night.

Jokes on branches, smiles in the glade,
Nature's punchlines, perfectly displayed.
Swinging on winds, they laugh and spin,
Giggles burst forth from within!

Embracing Vibrance Beneath the Sky

Under the shade, we giggle and play,
Colors twirl, making bright our day.
A pink polka dot on a leaf's green skin,
Like a dance-off, where do we begin?

Silly squirrels in vivid jackets,
Chasing shadows and goofy antics.
Racing each other, full of cheer,
Tumbling about, never any fear.

With confetti bursts and jolly cheers,
The landscape's humor tickles the years.
Beneath the sky, we sway and tease,
These shades of joy are sure to please!

Laughter hanging from every bough,
As nature chuckles, here and now.
A punchline hidden behind a fern,
Wait for it—oh, it's your turn!

Cascades of Colorful Delight

Rainbows tumble in a leafy spree,
Over giggles, what do you see?
Giant leaves wave, they sure look grand,
A friendly hand from nature's band.

Beneath the canopy, jokes abound,
Look at that robin, strutting around!
A riot of hues, no one's too shy,
Join the fun as laughter flies high.

Bubblegum pink meets lemony zest,
Nature's comedy, surely the best!
Swishing and swirling, what a delight,
Every color sparkles, shining bright.

So come now, join in the spree,
Let's paint the world with glee!
In this joyous, whimsical display,
Every moment's a bright bouquet!

Joyful Murmurs in the Canopy

In the treetops, secrets collide,
With every rustle, laughter's wide.
Whispers wrap round in jubilant glee,
A chortle here—oh, what a spree!

Oh, look! A wiggly worm in a hat,
Sipping on dew, oh, imagine that!
With vine-twirling friends, they're quite the sight,
Crafting new chuckles, all through the night.

Ticklish breezes zoom through the leaves,
Mischievous mouse in comic reprieves.
Painting the sky with laughter's embrace,
Every heartbeat a joyful space.

Follow the giggles, they lead the way,
To the heart of the forest, come out and play!
Nature's mirth is boundless, so grand,
In every nook, take your stand!

The Essence of Laughter

In the park, a squirrel darts by,
With acorns stacked, oh my!
He trips and rolls, what a sight,
Chasing tails in sheer delight.

The wind tickles, leaves take dance,
They giggle in a swaying prance.
A dog jogs, shakes his floppy ear,
While ducks quack jokes for all to hear.

Bouncing bubbles, a child's bright laugh,
Pop! And then, the aftermath.
Sticky fingers, candy bliss,
In this chaos, we find our bliss.

So let's embrace this playful glee,
In each moment, wild and free.
Life's a circus, come take a seat,
The essence of laughter, oh so sweet!

Ripples of Light

Sunlight splashes on the pond,
Frogs leap, forming a tiny bond.
A fish jumps high, gets a 'wow!'
A splashy show-off, take a bow!

Clouds tumble, giggling above,
Raindrops dance like a feathered dove.
They stick out their tongues, having fun,
Making puddles for everyone!

With each ripple, a laugh does soar,
A turtle peeks, then hides once more.
Funny faces, splashes in sight,
The world twinkles with pure delight.

In this frolic, bright and true,
The day wraps up with a giggly view.
If life gives you ripples, dance around,
For laughter's treasure is always found!

A Chorus of Whispers

Underneath the whispering trees,
The wind carries secrets with ease.
A bird critters, 'Have you heard?'
A squirrel's gossip, simply absurd!

The grass shakes, seems to agree,
With tiny giggles, oh so free.
A rabbit hops, nodding its head,
As the joke travels on, widespread.

The flowers snicker, colors so bright,
In a ruffled dance, they delight.
'What blooms today?' the daisies tease,
Sharing whispers on a playful breeze.

In this garden of tales, we laugh,
Stories spin like a joyful craft.
A chorus hums, a silly tune,
As happiness blooms from dawn till moon.

Gardens of Contentment

In the corner, a veggie patch laughs,
Carrots giggle, sharing their halves.
Tomatoes blush, in sunbeams bask,
Whispering secrets, 'We're up to the task!'

A chef nearby, with kitchen flair,
Trips on herbs, with style to spare.
Spices tumble, what a show!
A pinch of chaos, a dash of 'whoa!'

Bees buzz by with jiggly glee,
Pollinating joy, so happily.
They dance through blossoms, oh what a sight,
Creating sweetness through day and night.

In this patch, with such big dreams,
Every plant's bursting at the seams.
Gardens thrive with smiles galore,
Contentment found, forever more!

The Language of Nature

In the forest, trees can chat,
They giggle when we hear a brat.
Squirrels roll their acorn eyes,
As birds are singing silly lies.

The wind whispers secrets loud,
While flowers dance, feeling proud.
With every rustle, a joke's told,
Nature's comedy never gets old.

Bunnies hop with laughter bright,
Chasing shadows, what a sight!
Grasshoppers strum on tiny strings,
As the sun smiles and golden sings.

In this charming, leafy place,
Nature wears a funny face.
Together, join in the cheer,
For the jokes are crystal clear!

Enchanted Glades

In glades where giggles bounce and play,
The mushrooms wear hats in a quirky way.
With toadstools swaying to a beat,
Even the thorns leave us so sweet.

A rabbit with shades takes a stroll,
Telling tales that start to roll.
The trees clap as he does his dance,
While everyone else is caught in a trance.

But watch out! A squirrel might steal a snack,
With a cheeky grin and a little clack.
The ferns snicker, wave with glee,
As giggles bubble up from the creek.

Oh dear, what joy, what splendid fun,
In enchanted glades, we run and run.
Together we'll laugh, let worries flee,
In this magical spot, just you and me!

Shades of Feeling

In a patchwork quilt of colors bright,
Silly feelings take flight.
Joy in yellow, blue in surprise,
Emotions wear a funny disguise.

With tints of laughter painting blooms,
And cloudy pouts in the mushroom rooms.
Giggles rustle in the air,
While flowers tease with playful flair.

A tickle from the playful breeze,
Gives butterflies a chance to tease.
Colors dance, shades intertwine,
Beneath the sun, they brightly shine.

Mixing hues creates such cheer,
In the woods where joy is near.
With every shade, a smile spills,
In this land where laughter thrills!

The Spirit of Friendship

Among the branches, pals unite,
Sharing snacks, what a delight!
With owls giving winks and nods,
And porcupines pretending to be gods.

A turtle sings at a slow-paced tune,
Chasing shadows beneath the moon.
While foxes play hide and seek,
In the woods, every day's a cheeky peak.

Together they share tales so grand,
Of muddy puddles and jumping sand.
Raccoons laugh, what a crew,
In this world where friendships bloom anew.

Oh, what fun, oh, what jokes!
A family of quirky folks.
In the heart of nature's embrace,
Friendship beams with a funny face!

A Chorus of Colorful Moments

In gardens bright, laughter grows,
Where petals dance in sunlit shows.
A butterfly stuck on a sneeze,
Makes friends with bumblebees with ease.

Dancing leaves whisper silly tales,
Of jumping frogs and windy gales.
A squirrel spinning on a line,
Confetti dreams of lemon-lime.

Peeking through a friendly bush,
A hedgehog's snicker makes us hush.
As daisies wear their polka dots,
We giggle at the silly shots.

With every glance, chuckles flare,
Laughter blooms in crisp, fresh air.
In this bright world, fun intertwines,
A chorus sung by nature's signs.

Joy's Flourishing Embers

Amidst the petals, giggles blend,
As tulips tease, around they bend.
A worm who thinks he's on a roll,
Twists in soil, a wiggly goal.

Sunbeats play on grass's crown,
A picnic thief, a sneaky clown.
Chased by friends with playful flair,
He drops the crumbs of joy to share.

As daisies chit-chat with the breeze,
They tell the tales of silly Q's.
A ladybug wearing a tiny hat,
Winks at the world, then sits to chat.

So let this day be filled with cheer,
Where every moment's bright and clear.
Embers of fun ignite the soul,
In nature's laughter, we feel whole.

Uplifted Spirits Under a Gentle Sun

Under the sun, the giggles bloom,
A rabbit hops, finds a broom.
With every swish, leaves jump and sway,
In a whimsical, silly ballet.

A parade of ants holds the fort,
While crickets break into dance and sport.
Each blade of grass waves a hand,
Cheering on the merry band.

Clouds roll by, they peek and play,
Squinting down in a cloudy way.
A tickle of wind whispers their jokes,
As it teases the sprightly blokes.

As petals twirl in the gentle breeze,
Laughter echoes, hearts are at ease.
Bright spirits soar, lifted and free,
In the warmth of a sunny spree.

The Tingle of Awakening Colors

Awakening colors dance in line,
With silly socks, they sway and shine.
A flower shouts, "Look at me glow!"
While a daffodil steals the show.

The tickling breeze plays peek-a-boo,
As colors laugh, joyful and new.
A dog in shades joins the fun,
Chasing shadows, a wagging run.

In this vibrant, playful scene,
Turtles toss a salad green.
While daisies doodle on the ground,
Their funny shapes make laughter sound.

So let's embrace this lively spark,
Where echoes of giggles leave a mark.
In every hue, hapless and bold,
A symphony of stories unfolds.

Swaying with Sunshine

In the bright sun they dance and spin,
Tickling toes and wiggling grins.
They twirl and whirl, oh what a sight,
Chasing shadows, oh what delight!

Giggles mingle with the breeze,
Bouncing around like playful bees.
Watch them bounce, such carefree glee,
Nature's jesters, wild and free!

A Symphony of Color

A riot of hues, a playful spree,
Dressed in outfits of green and spree,
They shake and shimmy, dance in glee,
Turning drab into jubilee!

A polka dot curtain of orange and red,
Prancing around like they're being fed.
Each one's a character, with stories to tell,
In this vibrant circus, they do so well!

Radiant Echoes

Whispers of laughter fill the air,
As they catch giggles without a care.
They tumble and rustle, in grand display,
Turning the mundane into a play!

A chorus of chuckles in every sway,
Bouncing echoes brighten the day.
Cheeky and bright, they just can't resist,
In this funny ballet, they couldn't be missed!

Fields of Elation

A patchwork of sketches under the sun,
Joking around, oh what fun!
With a wink and a nod, they play along,
Making mischief like a silly song!

Each twist a laugh, every flop a cheer,
In the fields of humor, they have no fear.
Rolling in laughter, it's such a treat,
Nature's jest unfolds at our feet!

Petals of Delight

A flower snickered, petals wide,
It wore a hat, quite dignified.
Bees buzzed in, they'd lost their way,
Dancing round, they spun in play.

One daisy laughed, gave a great shout,
"Who's got nectar?" brought a pout.
The tulip winked, said, "I am sweet!"
While sniffing snails just took a seat.

A stormy gust made flowers sway,
Petals juggling in a fray.
A butterfly, with a pirate's eye,
Swiped a snack and flew up high.

And so they bloomed, each one a jest,
In the garden, they laughed the best.
Nature's humor, oh what a sight,
Each petal giggled through day and night.

The Dance of Gentle Breezes

Breezes twirled through the trees,
Tickling leaves with giggles and wheeze.
The branches bent, a comical sight,
As whispers turned to wild delight.

A squirrel mounted his acorn throne,
Proclaimed himself the king, alone!
The wind rolled past with a cheeky grin,
Sending him tumbling—oh, what a spin!

Up flew a kite, quite high in the air,
Tangled in branches, it zoomed without a care.
But the breeze just chuckled, a breezy tease,
"Hold tight, my friend, glide with ease!"

Each gust a prankster, full of cheer,
Shaking flowers, making them leer.
The world a stage, with laughter that frees,
In the frolicsome dance of gentle breeze.

Fragrant Moments

A rose scented cake, the garden's treat,
Served up with sprinkles for all it's sweet.
Frogs donned bow ties, leapt with class,
While honeysuckle feasted on grass.

The fragrance played peekaboo with the sun,
Mixing laughter, oh what fun!
A dandelion, brave as can be,
Called out, "Count me in, just wait and see!"

The daisies rallied, 'Let's have a blast!'
With aroma wars, they'd have a blast.
Mint brought its charm, vanilla soared,
In this aromatic world, they all adored.

Funny moments, fragrant air,
Sharing smiles without a care.
In nature's kitchen, the jokes would rise,
Filling hearts, oh what a surprise!

Tapestry of Bliss

In a garden bright, colors collide,
Creating a quilt that cannot hide.
Pansies giggling in shades of glee,
Said, "Join our party, come play with me!"

The sun wore glasses, chilling in style,
Brightening days with its warming smile.
The clouds donned capes, ready to fly,
As butterflies gathered, both shy and spry.

A ladybug hummed, leading the crew,
"Let's weave this day, just me and you!"
With each little stitch, their giggles burst,
In this tapestry, laughter was first.

The moon winked down, as night drew near,
Whispers of joy filled the air with cheer.
In this vibrant craft, they all found bliss,
In every stitch, a tender kiss.

A Journey of Wonder

In a forest where giggles bloom,
A squirrel wore a tiny costume.
He danced beneath the swaying trees,
Making friends with buzzing bees.

The rabbits twirled in silly pairs,
With floppy ears and boisterous stares.
They hopped like they were on a spree,
No one could stop their jubilee.

Acorns bounced like popcorn treats,
While chipmunks snacked on tasty sweets.
The sun peeked in, a cheerful sprite,
Chasing clouds on this funny flight.

The Comfort of Green

A garden full of laughter, they say,
Where veggies giggle and dance all day.
Tomatoes roll down a sunny mound,
While carrots giggle, turning round.

The lettuce flopped, declaring a truce,
As peas whispered, "This is no excuse!"
They played hide and seek with buzzing flies,
In this green haven, no one says goodbye.

Suddenly, a pickle popped up with glee,
"Join my party, come dance with me!"
Before you know it, the garden shook,
With veggies flirting like a storybook.

Harmony in the Air

The sky sang songs of fluffy delight,
With clouds that blinked and sparkled bright.
A breeze tickled the bushes wide,
As birds played tag, they took a glide.

The sun winked down, a playful tease,
While crickets bounced on buzzing keys.
A butterfly painted in colors bold,
Flipped and flopped like a tale retold.

With every rustle, the laughter grew,
A symphony of joy that everyone knew.
Nature's party, not to be missed,
Just listen close, you'll get the gist!

Sunlit Reveries

In a park where shadows play,
Sunbeams chase the clouds away.
Children giggle, racing around,
While ice cream drips to the ground.

A puppy pounced with the biggest grin,
Chasing his tail, where to begin?
He vaulted high, a furry baller,
Landing in puddles with a grand splatter.

The swings swayed as laughter soared,
A symphony of joy and rewards.
With each giggle, the world seemed right,
In this sunlit realm, pure delight.

Tenacious Hues Beneath the Canopy

In a dance of colors, bold and bright,
The trees wear outfits, quite a sight.
They rustle and giggle, whisper and sway,
Claiming they run the grand ballet.

With quirky hats and shoes so fine,
The branches play tricks, oh so divine.
Who knew tree limbs could be so spry?
They wave and twirl, reaching the sky.

A squirrel joins in with a little jig,
While owls hoot loud, dancing a big.
Underneath the canopy's playful cheer,
Nature's comedy is crystal clear.

In shades of green with splashes of fun,
The forest erupts, laughter has begun.
Join the frolic, don't be shy,
Underneath the hues, life's a sweet pie!

Frolic of Genial Shadows

Beneath the boughs where shadows prance,
The critters gather for a chance.
A game of tag, who'll win this round?
In giggles and squeaks, joy can be found.

The sun peeks through, like a nosy friend,
As leaf bits flutter and start to blend.
A dance of trolls, or shadows in flight,
Core cases of humor, oh what a sight!

A snail in a hurry, a turtle's retreat,
Both end up grinning at their small feat.
What an odd bunch, this merry team,
Basking in laughter, fulfilling their dream.

So come join the jive, the trees invite,
To laugh with the shadows, what pure delight!
In this frolic, let worries dissolve,
In the glow of the day, watch life evolve!

The Uplift of Nature's Caress

Oh what a tickle, this breeze on my nose,
The flowers laugh as their fragrance grows.
They wave goodbye to the passing cloud,
With petals dancing, they're feeling proud.

A cheeky butterfly flutters about,
Wearing stripes and a grin, creating a rout.
Chasing the wind, it dips and dives,
In this merry mood, it truly thrives.

The daisies chuckle, the violets cheer,
With nature's humor, nothing to fear.
Each gust a giggle, each rustle a jest,
In this comedy play, we are truly blessed.

A prank on a bee who forgot where to land,
Such silly antics, so perfectly planned!
With joy in abundance, let laughter sing,
In the uplifts of nature, find the joy it brings.

Paradise Found in the Green

In the thick of the wood, a treasure unfolds,
Where nature's reminders are surprisingly bold.
Laughter erupts from a bush so spry,
As critters enact their hilarious lie.

The toads are reciting a croaky tune,
While rabbits hop in a bright afternoon.
Each smile is spread with a delicate leaf,
Creating antics beyond belief!

A picnic of ants, with sandwiches tiny,
Sharing their snacks, oh so whiny.
Their tales of woe, about crumbs they lost,
Generate giggles, though they were tossed.

In paradise green, let humor reclaim,
With blunders and laughter, life is a game.
So dance with the flowers, skip with the breeze,
In this joyous forest, find life's sweet tease!

The Glow of Togetherness

In the park we sit and grin,
A squirrel steals our snack again.
We chase him round with squeaky glee,
Our laughter mixed with honeyed tea.

The sun spills gold from skies so bright,
As butterflies dance in delight.
With friends around, the world is free,
We're joking 'bout the bumblebee.

Each moment shared, a silly tale,
Of pranks and wiggles, we prevail.
With giggles loud and hearts so light,
Every mishap is pure delight.

So here's to us, a joyful crew,
With antics fresh, like morning dew.
Together we can face the day,
In this warm glow, we dance and play.

Petal-soft Memories

When daisies dance upon the ground,
We chase the bees that hum around.
Each step a skip, a frolic, fling,
Our laughter makes the robins sing.

Remember when we tripped and fell,
And rolled right into that old well?
We laughed until the stars appeared,
Those silly moments, loved and cheered.

Tiny hats upon our heads,
We fought with flowers, tossed like threads.
The petals twirled in laughter's breeze,
Our spirits soaring like the trees.

With every memory spun from glee,
We treasure times, just you and me.
In petal-soft, the past ignites,
And fills our days with pure delights.

Vistas of Laughter

Upon the hill we play the fool,
Pretending we're in a swimming pool.
With wild imaginations, we dive,
In vistas where our giggles thrive.

The clouds above, they never fret,
They glance and wonder, "What's up yet?"
We build a castle made of sand,
And swear it's the best in the land.

Our shadows dance in vibrant hues,
As we try out our funky shoes.
Each leap, a story we create,
With smiles that never hesitate.

So here we are, the jesters bold,
With laughter worth its weight in gold.
In this vast space, we jump and run,
Collecting memories, oh what fun!

The Gift of Nature

A flower gifts us with a wink,
We laugh at bugs that stop to drink.
With every stroll, nature's delight,
Turns boring days into pure flight.

The trees wear hats made out of moss,
We giggle hard, we're at a loss.
Caterpillars slow dance on leaves,
Their wobbly moves give us reprieves.

A pond reflects our mirrored glee,
As frogs perform a symphony.
With croaks that sound like silly songs,
The gift of nature hums along.

So let us cherish every sight,
Of giggles shared, our hearts so light.
With nature's wonders all around,
In joy and laughter, we are found.

Garden of Wishes

In a garden where giggles grow,
Wishing stones dance to and fro.
Bumblebees wear tiny hats,
Chasing butterflies with silly stats.

Daisies laugh with all their might,
Under the moon, what a sight!
The sun gets jealous, rolls his eyes,
While all the rabbits tell clever lies.

The Gentle Tread

On a path of candy canes,
Each step tickles like soft rains.
Squirrels waltz with acorn crowns,
And wear mismatched, silly gowns.

A gentle tread brings chuckles near,
As giggling flowers lend an ear.
With every skip, the mushrooms sway,
Wishing it were always play day.

Breezeless Adventures

Without a breeze, the kites are stuck,
Dancing in laughter, oh what luck!
Penguins slide down grassy hills,
Riding on snails as they have thrills.

Jellybeans hop and roll around,
While gummy worms make silly sounds.
They giggle and wiggle, what a show,
In this place where fun seeds grow!

A Tumble of Sunshine

A tumble of sunshine, oh what a day,
Chasing shadows that laugh and play.
With ticklish clouds floating high,
And the sun giving winks from the sky.

As raindrops slip on banana peels,
Laughter echoes like a spinning wheel.
In puddles, ducks dance with delight,
While frogs chant songs that feel just right.

Breezes of Abundance

Whispers in the air, oh so spry,
Dancing with laughter, trees wave hi,
A squirrel in a top hat strolls by,
Thinking he's the king, oh my oh my!

Sunshine giggles through branches wide,
A parade of odd frogs take a ride,
Pies in the sky, they cannot hide,
Nature's circus is open wide!

Juggling acorns, oh what a sight,
Grasshoppers croon under moonlight,
Wind makes faces, it's such delight,
Tickling the blooms, oh, what a flight!

Chasing shadows where jokes are spun,
Every tickle creates such fun,
On this stage, no one weighs a ton,
Laughter echoes, the day is won!

Melodies of the Heart

A duck in a bow tie sings a tune,
Swinging with frogs under a bright moon,
They all dance like a cartoon,
Turning the night into a festoon.

Bumblebees hum a jazzy refrain,
Jellybeans fall from the sky like rain,
Squirrels with trumpets go insane,
Grooving and jiving, oh what a gain!

Caterpillars strut with a flair,
In their tiny suits, they do declare,
That fungi on stage has flair to spare,
Underneath the stars, without a care!

Every giggle flutters in the breeze,
Where each soft cloud is like a tease,
Donuts and muffins, oh yes, please!
In this realm, nonsense is the keys!

Gentle Cascades

Down the slope, the giggles flow,
Mischievous laughter, a natural show,
Puddles invite all to come and go,
Slip and slide like a river's flow!

Butterfly ballet on the streams,
Twinkling like magical dreams,
Splashing water, oh how it gleams,
Nature concocts the best ice creams!

Jumping fish play hopscotch around,
While bubbles rise up from the ground,
Every plop makes a joyful sound,
As giggly gnomes start to abound!

In every ripple, laughter hides,
Frogs on lily pads take their rides,
In this world where joy collides,
With water's song, our spirit glides!

Illuminated Dreams

Twinkling stars wear silly hats,
As fireflies dance with playful spats,
A unicorn prances with cool cats,
In a moonlit land of cushy mats!

Clouds giggle as they change their shape,
Kites of candy swirl, escape,
While silly shadows start to drape,
Around the dreamers, joy takes shape!

Oh, the giggling trees whisper sweet,
Tickling the ground with every beat,
Where blueberry pies are a tasty treat,
In this land, all the dreams compete!

Laughter spills like a glittering stream,
As silly creatures join the theme,
In a world where all parties beam,
The night unfolds like a happy dream!

Scents of Awareness

A whiff of laughter fills the air,
Socks on heads, without a care.
Petunias giggle in their pots,
While snails slide by in silly knots.

Butterflies wear tiny hats,
Buzzing bees joke with the cats.
Every bloom blooms with delight,
As squirrels dance from morn till night.

The breeze tickles the nose,
As birds gossip in sweet prose.
They chirp about the garden's charm,
While worms groove beneath the farm.

In this world of quirky fun,
Nature's laughter has begun.
Come join the dance, don't you fret,
It's the best show you'll ever get!

A Burst of Color

Crayons spilled on grassy greens,
Flowers laugh in sunny scenes.
Pansies wear their polka dots,
While tulips join the silly plots.

Daffodils don silly shades,
Making jokes in sunny glades.
Roses blush, oh what a sight,
As they twirl in pure delight.

The sky is painted bright and bold,
Giggling clouds, tales untold.
Rainbows stretch in funny ways,
While puddles splash in playful plays.

A riot of hues dance in cheer,
Nature's laughter, oh so clear.
Join the fun, don't hesitate,
In this colorful, joyous state!

Browning Feathers

Feathers drift in a funny way,
Crows play cards, hip-hip-hooray!
Pigeons strut in fancy shoes,
While sparrows gossip morning news.

Hairdos made of frizz and fuzz,
Chickens dance and get a buzz.
Roosters crow in vibrant glee,
Claiming breakfast for their spree.

Ducks in bowties waddle past,
Practicing their slow-motion cast.
Every flap is full of grace,
In this feathered, funny race.

Nature loves to tease and play,
Join the feathers, come what may.
With every quack and happy shout,
Life's a game, without a doubt!

Glistening Horizons

Sunrise peeked with a cheeky grin,
Painting shades where dreams begin.
Horizons wink, oh what a view,
As the stars bid their adieu.

Clouds wear pajamas, fluffy and bright,
While the sun warms up with all its might.
Mountains giggle, valleys hum,
Nature plays its favorite drum.

Moonbeams bounce on the playful sea,
Dancing waves as happy as can be.
Lighthouses flash like disco lights,
Guiding sailors through the nights.

Come roam the paths where dreams reside,
With skies of blue as your joyful guide.
In this world of laughter and fun,
Dance beneath the glorious sun!

www.ingramcontent.com/pod-product-compliance
Lightning Source LLC
Chambersburg PA
CBHW070303120526
44590CB00017B/2550